PRAY LIKE JESUS
Learn to pray to God as Father

21-day Devotional Plan

*Derived from the full-length book
by the same title*

REALFAITH.COM

**By Mark Driscoll
and His Daughter Ashley Chase**

Pray Like Jesus: Learn to Pray to God as Father Devotional Plan
© 2021 by Mark Driscoll & Ashley Chase

ISBN: 978-1-7366834-8-4 (Paperback)
ISBN: 978-1-7366834-9-1 (E-book)

Unless otherwise indicated, Scripture quotations are from The Holy Bible, English Standard Version, copyright 2001 by Crossway Bibles, a publishing ministry of Good News Publishers. Used by permission. All rights reserved.

All emphases in Scripture quotations have been added by the author.

No part of this publication may be reproduced, stored in a retrieval system, or transmitted in any form by any means, electronic, mechanical, photocopy, recording, or otherwise, without the prior permission of the publisher, except as provided for by USA copyright law.

CONTENTS

DESCRIPTION. 1

REAL GROUPS 3

1. What is prayer?. 5
2. The Father Heart. 9
3. The Father Wound. 13
4. Father or Master? Slave or Son?. 17
5. Praying to the Father Through the Son by the Spirit. 21
6. Praying Fervently in Faith. 26
7. Praying Humbly in God's Will. 31
8. The Lord's Prayer Part 1: Religion, Rebellion, or Relationship. .35
9. The Lord's Prayer Part 2: Adoration, Worship, Provision,
   Confession, Intercession, Protection. 39
10. Gethsemane Part 1: The Road to the Garden. 44
11. Gethsemane Part 2: Thy Will Be Done. 48
12. Gethsemane Part 3: Pray Against Temptation. 53
13. The High Priestly Prayer Part 1: Pray For Yourself. 56
14. The High Priestly Prayer Part 2: Pray for Christians. 61
15. The High Priestly Prayer Part 3: Pray for Non-Christians. 67
16. When Did Jesus Pray? Part 1. 72
17. When Did Jesus Pray? Part 2. 75
18. Where Did Jesus Pray?. 78
19. How Did Jesus Pray? Part 1. 82
20. How Did Jesus Pray? Part 2. 86
21. Conclusion. 91

ABOUT PASTOR MARK, ASHLEY CHASE, AND REAL FAITH. 93

DESCRIPTION

Pray Like Jesus is a 21-day Bible-led journey designed to explain how prayer is talking to your Heavenly Father through Jesus' teaching about prayer as well as his own prayer life. *Pray Like Jesus* explores what prayer is, who God the Father is, how we should pray, what we should pray for, and when and where we should pray, giving practical steps towards building a prayer life like Jesus'.

This plan originated on the YouVersion Bible app and is derived from the full-length book by the same title. To purchase *Pray Like Jesus,* visit **RealFaith.com/Store**.

PRAY LIKE JESUS

21-DAY DEVOTIONAL

REAL GROUPS
WITH REAL FAITH

Faith that does not result in good deeds is not real faith.
-James 2:20, TLB

At Real Faith, we believe that the Word of God isn't just for us to read, it's to be obeyed. And living in community with fellow believers is one of the ways God the Father allows us to learn and grow to become more like His Son Jesus through the power of the Holy Spirit. We do this through something called Real Groups. Here are a few tips to start your own.

1. Invite

Invite your friends, neighbors, family, coworkers, and enemies, because they all need Jesus whether they know Him or not! Whether it's a group of men, women, families, students, or singles, explain that you'd like to start a weekly sermon based small group based on Pastor Mark Driscoll's sermons.

2. Listen to the sermon on realfaith.com or the Real Faith app

You can host a viewing party to watch Real Faith Live and discuss it all at once, or you can watch it separately and gather to discuss it at another time that works for the group.

3. Get into God's Word

PRAY LIKE JESUS

In addition to watching the sermon, make sure you and all group members have a study guide from realfaith.com for the current sermon series. There are questions for personal reflection as well as for groups that can guide your devotional times throughout the week. You can also sign up for Daily Devos at realfaith.com.

4. Gather together

Whether at someone's house, a public place, or through something like Zoom, meet weekly to discuss the sermon and what God taught you through it. The great thing about Real Groups is that you don't all have to be in the same location. You can talk about sermon takeaways, what stood out to you in the study guide, or what God taught you in His Word that week. Focus on personal application as much as possible.

5. Pray

When you gather, feel free to share prayer requests, pray for each other on the spot, and continue praying throughout the week. Prayer is a great unifying force that God gives us to strengthen His family.

6. Share

Send us photos, videos, testimonies, and updates of how your group is doing to hello@realfaith.com. You might even be featured on our Real Faith Live show!

There are plenty more resources to discover at realfaith.com/real-groups, as well. We will be praying for you and your group and look forward to hearing what God does through it.

21-DAY DEVOTIONAL

DAY 1
WHAT IS PRAYER?

Jeremiah 29:12 - Then you will call upon me and come and pray to me, and I will hear you.

Prayer. Does just reading that word make you feel at least a little bit guilty?

Talking about your prayer life often makes you feel scrutinized or nervous. It's the spiritual equivalent of talking about your diet or exercise—you know you could do better. You're easily embarrassed to talk about it or apologetic for your lack of consistency. Some don't know how to pray or don't pray enough; others only pray at the last minute, not unlike only dialing the police in the case of an emergency. We can't remember ever meeting anyone who thought they prayed often enough, earnestly enough, or faithfully enough.

Making matters worse, maybe you don't understand prayer, no one's ever told you how to pray, or like the kid in school who never really learned how to read, others just assume you know how to pray when you, in fact, do not and are a bit embarrassed to admit it.

Prayer is not something you have to do. Prayer is something that you get to do! God invites us to pray by promising in Jeremiah 29:12, "...call upon me and come and pray to me, and I will hear you."

In its most general sense, prayer simply means communicating with God. This can be done audibly as God hears our words, or silently as God knows our thoughts. Prayer is the primary way we engage in relationship with God, and just as communication is key to interpersonal relationships, it is vital to our relationship with God. That's what prayer is: having a conversation with God.

Moreover, because communication is designed to run two ways, prayer can include both speaking to God and hearing from God.

As the Father's child, your conversations with God with can be done anywhere and in a variety of ways, whether in a traditional posture of bent knees, bowed head, and clasped hands or in more natural ways, as when you're driving the car, mowing the yard, or shopping for groceries. You can journal your prayers or pray through the writing of songs or poetry. You can shout your prayers, or you can maintain a receptive silence, listening for the still, small voice of God. You can even use art and creativity as a way to pray.

No matter how or when you pray, the goal is always the same, to build your loving child-parent relationship with God. This concept has made more and more sense to me (Mark) as Grace and I parent our kids. One thing has remained constant from the time that our children were little to the present day when I now look up at Ashley's three brothers who have outgrown me: I did not much care what we did so long as they knew I loved them and we were building our relationship. When the boys were young, this meant a lot of wrestling, an infinite number of hours playing whiffle ball, and me frequently playing Goliath as they pretended to end my life in tribute to David. When the two girls were young, this meant playing board games, having countless tea parties, and more than a few expensive daddy dates.

21-DAY DEVOTIONAL

So long as they knew I loved them, we were together, and we were building our relationship, my joy came in seeing their joy. I wanted to be in their world, enjoying their company and capturing their heart. I not only loved our kids, but I also liked them—and still do. God the Father is like that with you, His child, but He's infinitely better in a way that only a perfect Dad could be.

Reflection:
1. Do you have a favorite way to pray (e.g. silently, out loud, alone, in a group, journaling, singing, etc.?)
2. How would you explain your prayer life in the past and present?
3. What changes would you like to make in your prayer life in the future?

NOTES

PRAY LIKE JESUS

21-DAY DEVOTIONAL

DAY 2
THE FATHER HEART

Psalm 8 - O Lord, our Lord, how majestic is your name in all the earth! You have set your glory above the heavens. Out of the mouth of babies and infants, you have established strength because of your foes, to still the enemy and the avenger. When I look at your heavens, the work of your fingers, the moon and the stars, which you have set in place, what is man that you are mindful of him, and the son of man that you care for him? Yet you have made him a little lower than the heavenly beings and crowned him with glory and honor. You have given him dominion over the works of your hands; you have put all things under his feet, all sheep and oxen, and also the beasts of the field, the birds of the heavens, and the fish of the sea, whatever passes along the paths of the seas. O Lord, our Lord, how majestic is your name in all the earth!

One night, when my oldest daughter Ashley was very little, I was undertaking our regular bedtime routine: worshipping together (despite my awful singing voice), cuddling, reading the Bible, catching up on the day, praying, and pressing the covers in around her, which we fondly called "tucking her in like a burrito."

As I prayed over her, the Holy Spirit showed up and, for the first time in my life, I finally understood prayer. With a big smile, she looked at me and said, "I am glad I have a daddy on earth and a Daddy in

Heaven who both love me. It's nice that I can talk to either of you anytime I want, and you will hear me and help me. Good night."

She smiled, closed her eyes, and went to sleep. For me, the Lord had just spoken through my little girl as He said He would, "You have taught children and infants to tell of your strength" (Psalm 8:2).

As I walked out of her room and turned off her light, I felt as if God had used her words to turn on a light inside me through that sacred moment with my sweetie pie. Three things have stuck with my soul ever since:

1. God shared His title of Father, or Dad, with me. This revelation brought an entirely new, meaningful weight to my role. I wanted to make sure that as she, and later her siblings, heard about God the Father that my love for them as their earthly father did not cause them to be confused or scared of Him since we shared the same title.
2. My daughter knew how to pray very naturally. For her, it was talking with a Dad who loved her. This type of prayer seemed far more personal, intimate, warm, and natural than the more religious and rote way I had wrongly viewed prayer. It is also exactly how Jesus taught us to pray—something we will explore in great detail throughout this book.
3. Not only was I Ashley's dad, but I was also the Father's child. God was not only her Dad but also mine. If I wanted to grow in prayer, I needed to stop focusing on religious people and their ways of praying. I needed to start learning from my children as they brought their needs, fears, and joys to me as a dad who loved

them and always had time for and interest in them. If my heart and mind could become more childlike, as Jesus taught, and focus more on getting to know my Dad than how to pray, odds are my prayer life would be more like my daughter's, which would be a good thing.

Ashley taught me a lot that day, and we're still learning together as we do ministry and get Bible teaching out about the Father's heart for all His sons and daughters.

Reflection:
1. What can we learn about prayer from kids?
2. If you are a parent, what can you teach your kids about prayer?
3. What observations come to mind when you think about relating to God the Father as kids who have a healthy and happy relationship with their dad?

NOTES

PRAY LIKE JESUS

21-DAY DEVOTIONAL

DAY 3
THE FATHER WOUND

Malachi 4:5-6 - "Behold, I will send you Elijah the prophet before the great and awesome day of the Lord comes. And he will turn the hearts of fathers to their children and the hearts of children to their fathers, lest I come and strike the land with a decree of utter destruction."

Matthew 27:46 - And about the ninth hour Jesus cried out with a loud voice, saying, "Eli, Eli, lema sabachthani?" that is, "My God, my God, why have you forsaken me?"

John 14:18 - "I will not leave you as orphans; I will come to you."

The final words of the Old Testament are about John the Baptizer: "His preaching will turn the hearts of fathers to their children, and the hearts of children to their fathers. Otherwise I will come and strike the land with a curse" (Malachi 4:5-6).

We tend to think of people in a variety of categories: gender, race, income level, education level, nationality, political party, age, marital status, and so on. God tends to think of people in two categories: those who are cursed and those who are blessed.

What causes the most cursing is fathers. God's final word was that families and nations are cursed for generations when fathers do not have a heart for their children, which in turn causes children not to have a heart for their fathers. The reason so many families are crumbling, along with churches and nations built on the family unit, is because a divided house falls, just as Jesus predicted.

Since we have three kinds of fathers, people can have three kinds of father wounds. A father wound is simply an unhealed hurt from a physical father, spiritual father, or father figure. These categories are not mutually exclusive, and someone can have multiple father wounds from multiple kinds of fathers.

Since no father is perfect, we are bound to have some degree of hurt and disappointment in one or more of these areas. For a moment, think of the most influential man or men in your life, whether he loomed large in his presence or absence, and ask yourself what was/is he like?

Coming to terms with the fact that fathers influence our lives no matter what kind of father they are is crucial in understanding how we communicate with our heavenly Father and relate to those around us. When we don't deal with the flaws in our relationships with our earthly fathers, we spend our whole lives trying to avoid making the same mistakes in our relationships. But in the process, we become so fixated on the issues that we repeat them instead of finding healing from them in prayer.

The father wound explains various misunderstandings of God the Father as each is either a projection or rejection of a man on earth onto the Father in heaven. This thinking is completely backward. We are not to begin our understanding of God the Father by looking at men on earth and assuming He is like them. Instead, we are to look to God the

21-DAY DEVOTIONAL

Father and judge other men on earth by the character and conduct of our Father in heaven.

To heal the father wound, we need to forgive the father on earth who hurt us and start spending time with our Father in heaven who can heal us. A father wound allows a failed earthly father to stand between you and your heavenly Father. Although He is there for you, you cannot see Him because your bitterness blocks your view. In this way, a wound is the spiritual equivalent of an eclipse where an earthly father blocks the light that shines on you from your heavenly Father. Forgiveness is how you release that man, remove that eclipse, and receive a new relationship with God as Father.

On the cross, one of Jesus' final seven words was, "why have you forsaken me?" (Matthew 27:46). At that moment, Jesus took your place. At that moment, Jesus took on Himself all your sin, and the Son of God was forsaken—or orphaned as Jesus used the words interchangeably—so that the Father could adopt you into the Forever Family. Jesus Christ was orphaned so that you could be adopted by a Father who will never abandon you or orphan you. The most secure relationship in all eternity is between God the Father and you, His child.

Reflection:
1. What is your relationship with your physical father, spiritual fathers, and father figures like? How have you projected these relationships onto your Heavenly Father?
2. Has God revealed any father wounds in your life? If so, list them and begin to process them with the Father.

PRAY LIKE JESUS

NOTES

21-DAY DEVOTIONAL

DAY 4
FATHER OR MASTER? SLAVE OR SON?

Galatians 4:3-7 - In the same way we also, when we were children, were enslaved to the elementary principles of the world. But when the fullness of time had come, God sent forth his Son, born of woman, born under the law, to redeem those who were under the law, so that we might receive adoption as sons. And because you are sons, God has sent the Spirit of his Son into our hearts, crying, "Abba! Father!" So you are no longer a slave, but a son, and if a son, then an heir through God.

Ephesians 2:3 - ...among whom we all once lived in the passions of our flesh, carrying out the desires of the body and the mind, and were by nature children of wrath, like the rest of mankind.

When our daughter Ashley was first born, her mother and I held her, prayed for her, and kept telling her that we were her parents. Instinctively, we knew that she needed to know who we were and that we were there to love her, protect her, and provide for her.

What is true when we are born is also true when we are born again. The first thing we need to know is who our Parent is, "because you are sons, God has sent the Spirit of his Son into our hearts, crying, 'Abba! Father!' So you are no longer a slave, but a son, and if a son, then an heir through God" (Galatians 4:6-7). The storyline of the Bible is that we are born as "slaves of sin" and "by nature children of wrath" (Ephesians 2:3). Simply stated, we were born with Satan as our father, the same as the religious leaders Jesus rebuked, and we are enslaved by sin and death. When the Holy Spirit gives you a new heart and made you a new person, He also gives you a new Father and new freedom from sin.

Do you relate to God as Master or Father?

Many people struggle with prayer because they wrongly view God as Master. If God is mean, unloving, controlling, harsh, and uses you, then running to Him to build a loving, intimate relationship by inviting Him into every aspect of your life is the very last thing you would do. Conversely, if God is your Father, that is the very thing you should do.

Do you see yourself as a slave or a son?

A son or daughter with a father lives from their identity. Conversely, a slave with a master lives for their identity. If they perform well and please the master, they are rewarded. If they fail to perform well for the master, they are punished. A slave has to earn their identity and can lose it at any time. This reality causes great pressure to perform, be perfect, and not disappoint in any way.

Many people—especially if they had a perfectionist, religious, demanding, military-minded, or competitive parent—are hardwired to believe in a works-based identity. A works-based identity is earned and can be lost. The opposite is a grace-based identity, which is not achieved by you but received by you as a gift from the Father given by your Big Brother Jesus that cannot be lost.

Consider Jesus Christ, the Son of God. Having spent the first roughly thirty years of His life obeying His parents as a kid and working a carpentry job with His earthly father as a young man, Jesus began

21-DAY DEVOTIONAL

His public ministry by being baptized. Before Jesus had seemingly preached a sermon, healed the sick, or performed a miracle, God the Father spoke from heaven saying, "You are my beloved Son; with you I am well pleased" (Luke 3:22). In the very next chapter, Satan shows up and says two times, "If you are the Son of God," then you need to prove and achieve it by doing something (Luke 4:3,9). Jesus, by faith, believed who the Father said He was as Son, lived from that identity, and walked in spiritual victory.

As a dad, no matter what our kids do, I am still their dad who loves them, who wants to be a blessing to their life, and who lifts burdens, "When we were children, were enslaved to the elementary principles of the world....God sent forth his Son...so that we might receive adoption as sons" (Galatians 4:3-5).

Reflection:

1. Do you view God as Father or Master? Do you see yourself as a son or a slave?
2. How do these views affect your prayers?

NOTES

PRAY LIKE JESUS

21-DAY DEVOTIONAL

DAY 5
PRAYING TO THE FATHER THROUGH THE SON BY THE SPIRIT

Luke 11:1 - Now Jesus was praying in a certain place, and when he finished, one of his disciples said to him, "Lord, teach us to pray, as John taught his disciples."

Luke 10:21-22 - In that same hour he rejoiced in the Holy Spirit and said, "I thank you, Father, Lord of heaven and earth, that you have hidden these things from the wise and understanding and revealed them to little children; yes, Father, for such was your gracious will. All things have been handed over to me by my Father, and no one knows who the Son is except the Father, or who the Father is except the Son and anyone to whom the Son chooses to reveal him."

Mark 14:36 - And he said, "Abba, Father, all things are possible for you. Remove this cup from me. Yet not what I will, but what you will."

1 Timothy 2:5 - For there is one God, and there is one mediator between God and men, the man Christ Jesus...

1 Thessalonians 5:17 - ...pray without ceasing...

In Luke 11:1, the disciples say to Jesus, "Lord teach us to pray," and

PRAY LIKE JESUS

Jesus responds in Luke 11:13, "If you then, who are evil, know how to give good gifts to your children, how much more will the heavenly Father give the Holy Spirit to those who ask him!".

Jesus' answer to the request "Teach us to pray" is about receiving the gift of the Holy Spirit, because while Trinitarian prayer is directed to the Father it is empowered by the Holy Spirit.

The Holy Spirit actually teaches us how to pray and Jesus himself prayed by the Spirit in Luke 10:21-22. This prayer of Jesus is described as "rejoicing in the Holy Spirit," indicating that the Son's prayer to the Father is conducted in the joyful power of the Holy Spirit. This is a beautiful description of worshipful prayer that shows us how the Spirit empowers us to pray.

In Mark 14:36, Jesus prays, "Abba, Father, all things are possible for you. Remove this cup from me. Yet not what I will, but what you will."

This prayer shows us both Jesus' relational intimacy with God (calling him "Abba," which means something akin to "Daddy") and his submission to the Father's authority and will. In this example we learn two things: prayer to the Father should always be respectful but need not be formal.

Some of us are just way too serious with our prayers. I don't mean that prayer isn't serious business. I just mean we can wrongly think that if we pray in certain ways and with certain speech, God will be more inclined to hear us. But God is our Abba Father, our Dad. He wants to hear us, to answer us, and to help us. He doesn't require any more formalized rituals than any other loving daddy would.

I'm a dad of five kids. When wanting to go swimming, they don't

21-DAY DEVOTIONAL

approach me, saying, "Dearest Father, I beseechest thou to swimmeth with me because of thine deep mercies." They just say, "Dad, wanna swim?" They don't have to hem and haw, don't have to make a fifteen-minute speech, don't have to be uptight. They know that I love them and that they have the freedom to ask me for things.

We also need to remember that prayer is not telling God something he doesn't already know. You can't surprise God! My kids often tell me things that I already know, but their telling me is about talking to me, about experiencing relational intimacy with me. It's about the experience of me loving them, serving them, helping them, instructing them, caring for them. Conversation is key to all relationships.

When you have a problem or a concern, take it to the Father and talk about it with Him, just as Jesus did. 1 Timothy 2:5 informs us that "there is one God, and there is one mediator between God and men, the man Christ Jesus." So when we pray to the Father, we are praying by and in the power of the Spirit living in us, and we are praying through the power of Jesus Christ living for us.

As we seek to pray through the Son, we should seek to pray as the Son prayed. One thing we notice as we look through the Gospels for instances of Jesus praying is that he didn't exactly devote a large amount of time to direct teaching on prayer. Rather, we find that Jesus' direction on prayer is woven throughout his life and teaching. His prayers and his teachings on prayer are part of the fabric of His day-to-day life and ministry.

Jesus perfectly embodies the command of 1 Thessalonians 5:17: "pray without ceasing." Praying without ceasing means we don't have to put on our burlap Jedi robe, climb up a high mountain, get in the lotus position, drink decaf oolong tea, and say "om." We don't have to do that.

To pray like Jesus means living a prayerful life, where prayer is a constant and recurring habit like breathing, in our life lived in the Spirit. So we get out of bed and pray. We eat breakfast and pray. We get in the shower and pray. We get in the car and pray. We go to work and pray. We go shopping and pray. We study and pray. We clean out the garage and pray. Every day and in all facets of our day, we have the great privilege of getting to talk to our Father.

Reflection:
1. Spend some time in prayer today, and before you do ask invite the Holy Spirit to help you learn how to pray to God as Father from your heart, thanking Jesus for interceding for you to bring your prayers to the Father.
2. Think about a good father you know, and how they interact and converse with their child. What can you learn from them about conversing with your Father through prayer?

NOTES

21-DAY DEVOTIONAL

DAY 6
PRAYING FERVENTLY IN FAITH

Matthew 21:22 - "And whatever you ask in prayer, you will receive, if you have faith."

Luke 18:1 - And he told them a parable to the effect that they ought always to pray and not lose heart.

1 Corinthians 13:7 - Love bears all things, believes all things, hopes all things, endures all things.

Once we know what prayer is and how it relates to our relationship with God the Father, the next logical question is, "How should we pray?".

In Matthew 21:22, Jesus says, *"And whatever you ask in prayer, you will receive, if you have faith."*

Start with faith. We need to have faith that God exists, that he loves us, that he wants to take care of us, that he hears us, and that he wants us to have all we need. We need to have faith that the Spirit is teaching us to pray. We need to have faith that Jesus has died to forgive our sins, making us children whose prayers the Father chooses to hear.

Like all dads, God reserves three potential answers to all prayers: Yes, No, or Later. Sometimes we pray for things and we lament, "God didn't answer my prayer." But He did. He just said no. "No" is an answer.

21-DAY DEVOTIONAL

Some years ago, it was bedtime in my house, and three of my kids made requests. First kid comes up and says, "Dad, I'm hungry, can I have some grapes?" Yes. That's a do-able request. The next kid approached and says, "Dad, I'm thirsty, can I have a Coke?" No. There's no bedtime Coke. You don't have to stay up to study for mid-terms, you're six. Have some water. The next kid comes up and says, "Dad, I really enjoyed swimming with you today, can we go swimming again right now?" Later. We'll swim again. But not at ten o'clock at night. Right now, it's time for bed.

Three kids, three requests. I don't love any of them any less than the others. All three are my children whom I love and want to please. But based on the requests and the timing of the requests, they got three different answers. And that's how God answers us: Yes, No, or Later.

One of the simplest ways to pray in faith is to pray with the belief that God hears our prayers but that not getting what we want doesn't mean God isn't answering. Keep praying! Don't just pray once and move on.

Luke 18:1 reads, "And he told them a parable to the effect that they ought always to pray and not lose heart." Have you been praying for something for a long time that you believe is in God's will? Keep praying.

Why?

First, because you'll keep hoping. Fervent prayer keeps your heart inclined toward God and his blessings. The communication of prayer deepens your love for God, and 1 Corinthians 13:7 tells us that true love always hopes.

Second, fervent prayer will maintain a willingness in you to grow and be changed. Once you stop praying, you stop caring. But if you keep praying, your heart will grow more and more tender toward the things of God.

Third, if you keep praying you keep loving. If you keep praying for people, you will grow in love for people. If you keep praying for God's help and blessings in your life, you will grow in love for God.

So, if you're single and you are called to marriage, keep praying for your future spouse. Doing this is not only a great gift to your future partner, it also helps guard your own heart against temptation while you wait.

If you need a job, keep praying for one and seeking until your prayer is answered by God. If you are sick, keep praying for healing until you are healed in this life or taken home to be perfectly healed in God's kingdom.

Wait and pray in hope, and this hopeful, fervent expectancy will conform your heart to the will of God whatever his answer might be to your prayer.

God isn't sitting back waiting until we do a good job, withholding his love and provision from us until we have earned it. He loves us already and doesn't want us to withhold our hearts from him.

Please don't think your concerns are too little for God. God is your Father and, like any parent who really loves their child, no request is too small. Your Father is always listening to your requests and always willing to help you.

Reflection:

1. Is there anything that you believe is in God's will but that you have stopped praying about? If so, spend some time praying for that person or thing again today.
2. What thing do you struggle to trust God with in your life? Spend some time today discussing that with the Lord today, as well as discussing your fears about it with Him.

<u>NOTES</u>

PRAY LIKE JESUS

21-DAY DEVOTIONAL

DAY 7
PRAYING HUMBLY IN GOD'S WILL

John 16:23-24 - In that day you will ask nothing of me. Truly, truly, I say to you, whatever you ask of the Father in my name, he will give it to you. Until now you have asked nothing in my name. Ask, and you will receive, that your joy may be full.

Luke 18:9-14 - He also told this parable to some who trusted in themselves that they were righteous, and treated others with contempt: "Two men went up into the temple to pray, one a Pharisee and the other a tax collector. The Pharisee, standing by himself, prayed thus: 'God, I thank you that I am not like other men, extortioners, unjust, adulterers, or even like this tax collector. I fast twice a week; I give tithes of all that I get.' But the tax collector, standing far off, would not even lift up his eyes to heaven, but beat his breast, saying, 'God, be merciful to me, a sinner!' I tell you, this man went down to his house justified, rather than the other. For everyone who exalts himself will be humbled, but the one who humbles himself will be exalted."

Sometimes we wonder how to understand Jesus' words in John 16:23-24, "Ask and you will receive," and we're thinking, "Well, I asked, but I didn't receive. What's going on?"

What's usually going on is that we are not asking for something that is in accordance with God's will. What is God's will? Read your

PRAY LIKE JESUS

Bible. God wants you to grow, so pray that God will grow you. God wants you to pray for your enemies, so you pray for your enemies. God wants you to help the poor, so you pray for the poor.

Some of us pray against God's will. God will not answer prayers that are against His will. If, for example, you are praying for a sinful romantic relationship to be blessed, or a sinful business decision to be blessed, then you are not praying in God's will.

Those are bad prayers. It's like asking God to help you sin better. He's not going to say yes to that. Those are not prayers uttered is in "Jesus' name." In prayer, God changes our will to align with His so that He can bless our request that is in accordance with His desires.

What does it mean to pray to the Father in the name of Jesus? It means that we are not asking for things that run contrary to the honor of Jesus or that come from a place of disobedience to Jesus.

Sometimes we personally are not in accordance with God's will. Jesus shares a fascinating parable in Luke 18 about two guys going up to the temple to pray. One guy is super religious and very determined to create performance art out of his prayer. He prays arrogantly and loudly in essence, "I thank you, God, that I'm not a disgusting loser like all these other guys." And he refers to the other guy and says, "I especially thank you that I'm not like this guy." And that guy had to be thinking, "Hey, wait a minute."

This guy's whole prayer is about how awesome he thinks he is, and how much better he is than everybody else. Reading his prayer, it's a lot of I, I, I, and me, me, me.

But the other guy's prayer consists simply and succinctly and humbly of this: "God, be merciful to me, a sinner!" He is honest about his state before God. He's not seeking people's approval; he's seeking God's help.

Jesus said, "I tell you, this man went down to his house justified, rather than the other. For everyone who exalts himself will be humbled, but the one who humbles himself will be exalted."

That guy didn't pray long and he didn't pray like an expert. But he prayed respectfully and humbly, and God honored his prayer.

Some of us are sometimes praying for people in a very arrogant way. "Lord, help this person learn as much I have." "Lord, make this person see things the way I do." "Lord, show this person how great I am."

Those are awful, arrogant prayers.

God honors a humble heart, so pray humbly, with the acknowledgment that you are a sinner saved by grace, that God is in control and you are not, and that no amount of self-righteousness or prayerful performance will merit you anything. God is good and we do not need to manipulate Him to be good. God is impressive, but He's not impressed by us.

Reflection:

1. Before you spend time in prayer today, begin by asking God if your desires and requests are in line with His will for you. Then, only pray for those things that you are convinced are God's will for you.
2. Spend some time today in prayer focused on asking God to forgive any sin in your life. Also pray for the religious people who have caused you pain and harm, that God would forgive them too.

PRAY LIKE JESUS

NOTES

21-DAY DEVOTIONAL

DAY 8
THE LORD'S PRAYER PART 1:
RELIGION, REBELLION, OR RELATIONSHIP

Matthew 6:5-15 - "And when you pray, you must not be like the hypocrites. For they love to stand and pray in the synagogues and at the street corners, that they may be seen by others. Truly, I say to you, they have received their reward. But when you pray, go into your room and shut the door and pray to your Father who is in secret. And your Father who sees in secret will reward you. And when you pray, do not heap up empty phrases as the Gentiles do, for they think that they will be heard for their many words. Do not be like them, for your Father knows what you need before you ask him. Pray then like this: 'Our Father in heaven, hallowed be your name. Your kingdom come, your will be done, on earth as it is in heaven. Give us this day our daily bread, and forgive us our debts, as we also have forgiven our debtors. And lead us not into temptation, but deliver us from evil.' For if you forgive others their trespasses, your heavenly Father will also forgive you, but if you do not forgive others their trespasses, neither will your Father forgive your trespasses."

The world's most famous prayer from Jesus Christ is a snapshot of His relationship with His Father. Most of us are at least cursorily familiar with the Lord's Prayer. You've probably said it at some point in your life at least once, and many of us have it memorized. It's been set to music, recited in worship services, and even plastered on all kinds of products. Its simplicity, coupled with our familiarity with it, has tempted us to forget what great teaching the prayer is for us and just how great a gift it is to us.

The Lord's Prayer itself only takes up one short paragraph (just four short lines, depending on the translation). In its context, however, this whole passage constitutes Jesus' message instructing us on how to begin or deepen our parent-child relationship with God.

In Matthew 6:5-8, Jesus prefaces His teaching on how we should pray by first telling us how we should not pray. There are two groups that Jesus highlights as examples of how not to pray: the Pharisees and the Gentiles. In our day, we would consider these groups the religious and the rebellious, respectively.

Jesus was pointedly clear that we should not look to religious people for lessons on prayer. Indeed, while some religions and religious people may seem very pious and serious, Jesus is emphatic that this type of prayer is a problem because it diminishes our relationship with God, which defeats the entire goal of praying. Religious prayer is typically a performance for the approval of a human audience; it is heaping up empty phrases and big words into lengthy prayers as if God needs to be informed or compelled. You don't have to wear the Father down as if He didn't hear you the first time or just needs some extra convincing as if prayer was a stick, and He was a piñata.

On the other hand, the Gentiles "heap up empty phrases." These are trite, pithy statements that people who don't know God echo from other people who don't know God. Examples include, "when God closes

21-DAY DEVOTIONAL

a door He opens a window" from the book of 1 Nowhere 2:3, and, "You just need to send out good thoughts so that the universe will bless you," which is a direct quote from 2 Nonsense 6:66. God's not broken. Neither is He stingy. God is a good Father who knows what we, the kids He loves, need.

The third option is to be like a child. Christian prayer is to be humble, simple, respectful, sincere, and relational; it includes both speaking to and listening to God. By teaching us the Lord's Prayer, Jesus was not telling us what to say, as if His words were to be repeated over and over like an old record stuck in a groove. Instead, He says, "Pray like this." His prayer, then, is a model of prayer that, by the power of the indwelling Holy Spirit, we can learn from as our own prayer life matures.

From this prayer, it is clear that Jesus has a relationship with His Father, loves His Father, trusts His Father to provide, and honors His Father just like a kid with a good dad. And His Father sees His heart posture and lovingly hears and answers, just as He does with us.

Reflection:

1. Do you tend to be more religious or rebellious?
2. How can you focus more on your relationship with God as Father instead?

PRAY LIKE JESUS

NOTES

21-DAY DEVOTIONAL

DAY 9
THE LORD'S PRAYER PART 2:
ADORATION, WORSHIP, PROVISION, CONFESSION, INTERCESSION, PROTECTION

Matthew 6:5-15 - "And when you pray, you must not be like the hypocrites. For they love to stand and pray in the synagogues and at the street corners, that they may be seen by others. Truly, I say to you, they have received their reward. But when you pray, go into your room and shut the door and pray to your Father who is in secret. And your Father who sees in secret will reward you. And when you pray, do not heap up empty phrases as the Gentiles do, for they think that they will be heard for their many words. Do not be like them, for your Father knows what you need before you ask him. Pray then like this: 'Our Father in heaven, hallowed be your name. Your kingdom come, your will be done, on earth as it is in heaven. Give us this day our daily bread, and forgive us our debts, as we also have forgiven our debtors. And lead us not into temptation, but deliver us from evil.' For if you forgive others their trespasses, your heavenly Father will also forgive you, but if you do not forgive others their trespasses, neither will your Father forgive your trespasses."

The Lord's Prayer is a guide for how we should pray, and there are 6 elements that Jesus models for us to mimic.

"Our Father in Heaven": Adoration

The Lord's Prayer begins with the phrase Our Father. In these two simple terms are two towering truths. One, to be a Christian is to have God the Father lovingly adopt you to be His beloved child. Two, to be a Christian is to have a new spiritual church family with other brothers and sisters who also call on God together as our Father. As a Christian, you cannot be healthy unless you have both a relationship with God as Father and a church as a family.

"Hallowed Be Your Name. Your Kingdom Come, Your Will Be Done, on Earth as It Is in Heaven": Worship

Every day, the prayers we pray, words we speak, and decisions we make either invite the kingdom of God down into our lives or pull the kingdom of hell up into our lives. In any battle, secure and reliable communication channels are absolutely essential.

Worship includes music and singing songs, but it is much more than this. It is also about living lives that do God's will. Worship is praying for the kingdom to come, and then living as a citizen of that kingdom out of love for King Jesus. Prayer is how we align ourselves with God's will and position ourselves to help build God's kingdom.

"Give Us This Day Our Daily Bread": Provision

This portion of the prayer allows us to ask for practical things in life. You need food to eat, water to drink, and a place to live. For those things to get paid for, you also need a job and sufficient health to work it. God knows you have these needs, and when you ask Him, you are building your relationship. Your needs are not a burden. You are a blessing to your Father, just as children are a blessing to their parents.

21-DAY DEVOTIONAL

"Forgive Us Our Debts": Confession

This section of the prayer reminds us of our sinful state in the light of God's holiness, our debt to God. Both sins of omission—not doing what we should do—and sins of commission—doing things we shouldn't do—are accruing debt to God.

But it also reminds us that total forgiveness of our entire debt—past, present, and future—is available through Jesus! "Forgive us our debts" is an incredible acknowledgment of God's grace. God can and will forgive our entire spiritual debt. (And He has!) This reality welcomes us to pray for forgiveness with confidence and thanksgiving.

"As We Also Have Forgiven Our Debtors": Intercession

Forgiveness is a gift God gives to us, intending that we then share it with others. God's forgiven people should be godly, forgiving people. This truth does not mean that we ignore, diminish, or even excuse their sin. It doesn't mean we accept it or approve it. It doesn't mean that we trust them, or that in the future we remain relationally close to them. Forgiveness takes one person, but reconciliation takes two, so all we can do is our part.

The Greek word most used for forgiveness quite literally means to let it go. In choosing to forgive, we are saying, "I wish God's best for you. I give up my right to seek vengeance or justice. I leave your future in God's hands." The test of whether you have forgiven someone is blessing them. When someone acts like an enemy, and we forgive and bless them, we are treating them the way that God treated us when we were acting as His enemies. On the cross, where those who hated him had hung him to die, Jesus prayed in Luke 23:34, *"Father, forgive them, for they know not what they do."*

"Lead Us Not into Temptation, but Deliver Us from Evil": Protection

Sin is real. The devil and his demons are real. The world is filled with evil and fraught with temptation. God's people cannot afford to be foolish or naïve.

While we can and should pray defensively for forgiveness when we sin, we should also pray offensively—in advance—before temptation comes and evil lurks. Of course, our Father never tempts us to sin, but in this portion of the Lord's Prayer, Jesus is saying that we should agree with God's desire that we not bow to temptation and enter into evil.

Praying that God would protect us from temptation is just another extension of praying for God's will to be done. It is saying, "God, I agree with you, and I don't want to walk away from you in disobedience."

Reflection:
1. How can you incorporate these 6 elements of the Lord's Prayer into your own prayer life?
2. Do you truly believe that you are forgiven? Is there anyone that you have not truly forgiven and need to get some time alone with God to work through a process whereby you can truly forgive them from the heart? If so, consider journaling about this process of forgiveness.
3. In what area(s) of your life do you need to be praying offensively or proactively against temptation and evil?

21-DAY DEVOTIONAL

NOTES

PRAY LIKE JESUS

DAY 10
GETHSEMANE PART 1: THE ROAD TO THE GARDEN

Matthew 26:36-46 - Then Jesus went with them to a place called Gethsemane, and he said to his disciples, "Sit here, while I go over there and pray." And taking with him Peter and the two sons of Zebedee, he began to be sorrowful and troubled. Then he said to them, "My soul is very sorrowful, even to death; remain here, and watch with me." And going a little farther he fell on his face and prayed, saying, "My Father, if it be possible, let this cup pass from me; nevertheless, not as I will, but as you will." And he came to the disciples and found them sleeping. And he said to Peter, "So, could you not watch with me one hour? Watch and pray that you may not enter into temptation. The spirit indeed is willing, but the flesh is weak." Again, for the second time, he went away and prayed, "My Father, if this cannot pass unless I drink it, your will be done." And again he came and found them sleeping, for their eyes were heavy. So, leaving them again, he went away and prayed for the third time, saying the same words again. Then he came to the disciples and said to them, "Sleep and take your rest later on. See, the hour is at hand, and the Son of Man is betrayed into the hands of sinners. Rise, let us be going; see, my betrayer is at hand."

What someone does in the final moments of their life reveals who or what they care most about. As Jesus approached the end of His last day, He stopped to spend an entire night in prayer. Jesus' actions reveal

21-DAY DEVOTIONAL

that meeting with the Father in prayer was His highest priority.

Reading Jesus' Gethsemane Prayer is spiritually overwhelming, just as it was physically overwhelming for Jesus. Gethsemane means an oil press, and an oil press stood amid a field of olive trees where it was used to press the oil from the fruit by crushing it. John 18:1 reveals that an olive grove, or garden, was in this place where Jesus prayed. There, Jesus' soul would be pressed until it was crushed, and heartfelt prayer poured forth.

The night road to the Garden of Gethsemane was dark. Foreboding, it was littered with the heartbreak of betrayal and abandonment. The air was thick with pain and angst. At that moment, the weight of the world came on Jesus. He carried the sin of humanity to the cross, to the Place of the Skull looming on the horizon.

Jesus was fully aware of where His ministry was going, foretelling the manner of His murder. The only thing worse than marching into a deadly assault is knowing the outcome well in advance and marching forward anyway.

From that time Jesus began to show His disciples that he must go to Jerusalem and suffer many things from the elders and chief priests and scribes, and be killed, and on the third day be raised. —Matthew 16:21

Maybe you know what it's like to see that devastating moment just hanging over you. Have you had your Gethsemane moment? Were you overwhelmed by what was happening to you, feeling lonely because of abandonment and betrayal, helpless to change your fate, and sensing there was no way you were going to make it?

PRAY LIKE JESUS

When your spouse says, "I'm leaving," when the doctor says, "It's cancer," when the nurse says, "You've miscarried," when your sibling says, "Dad died, and he didn't know Jesus," what do you do? What you don't need to do on those days is pretend. Don't pretend that life is easy, and life is good. It's okay to say life is complicated and sometimes very, very painful.

In His moment of dying, Jesus didn't distrust, doubt, deny, or disregard God. Instead, He desired God. So, He prayed. Even Jesus needed to pray!

When you are sick, lonely, hurting, and in need, you need to talk to God. Even sinless, perfect Jesus needed to talk to the Father. If Jesus needed to pray in His Gethsemane moment, you need to pray in yours.

Reflection:

1. Do you pray to get from God or to get God?
2. In your life, what has been your Gethsemane moment(s)? How did you respond?

NOTES

21-DAY DEVOTIONAL

DAY 11
GETHSEMANE PART 2: THY WILL BE DONE

Matthew 26:36-46 - Then Jesus went with them to a place called Gethsemane, and he said to his disciples, "Sit here, while I go over there and pray." And taking with him Peter and the two sons of Zebedee, he began to be sorrowful and troubled. Then he said to them, "My soul is very sorrowful, even to death; remain here, and watch with me." And going a little farther he fell on his face and prayed, saying, "My Father, if it be possible, let this cup pass from me; nevertheless, not as I will, but as you will." And he came to the disciples and found them sleeping. And he said to Peter, "So, could you not watch with me one hour? Watch and pray that you may not enter into temptation. The spirit indeed is willing, but the flesh is weak." Again, for the second time, he went away and prayed, "My Father, if this cannot pass unless I drink it, your will be done." And again he came and found them sleeping, for their eyes were heavy. So, leaving them again, he went away and prayed for the third time, saying the same words again. Then he came to the disciples and said to them, "Sleep and take your rest later on. See, the hour is at hand, and the Son of Man is betrayed into the hands of sinners. Rise, let us be going; see, my betrayer is at hand."

Jesus begins His Gethsemane prayer with these haunting words: "My Father, if it be possible, let this cup pass from me; nevertheless, not as I will, but as you will" (Matthew 26:39). In this first of three prayers in the garden, Jesus humbly and earnestly made His request known that He preferred that the cup of suffering and wrath to be taken from Him.

Every moment of every day, sinners continue rebelling while thinking they are getting away with everything. The truth is, sinners get away with nothing but instead store up everything: "But because of your hard and impenitent heart you are storing up wrath for yourself on the day of wrath when God's righteous judgment will be revealed" (Romans 2:5). The word picture is sobering. Imagine in God's presence an uncountable number of cups, each with a person's name on it. Every time they sin, their cup of wrath fills up more and more. Either you drink that cup or Jesus drinks it for you.

Having a relationship with Jesus means praying to make our requests known to God and then asking Him not only to have His way but also to transform us so that our way matches His. We might not start there, but we get there by praying until we pray the surrender prayer "as you will."

Jesus prays this a second time, not because God didn't hear but because He is reminding Himself to continually submit to God's sovereign care.

Are you willing to trust God that much? It's okay to pray, "I'm single, and I'd like to be married" if you also pray, "Your will be done." It's okay if you're married to pray for a child if you also pray, "Your will be done." God writes the story we call our life.

For the third time, Jesus prays for God's will to be done. The subtle implication is not that Jesus merely prayed the same prayer three times, but that he only prayed it three times. He simply didn't have enough time to pray it any longer.

Some suffering has a known expiration date like Jesus' suffering, but some seems to go on endlessly. The question of God's sovereignty and goodness amid suffering is a popular and valid one, but when seeking an answer, we must keep in mind that Jesus suffered most of all. He was betrayed, forsaken, martyred, ridiculed, and mocked—and He was God. Like Jesus, our lives have a purpose in God's eyes, and the Father's timing is perfect. Praying in a way that invites the kingdom down helps fix our eyes on eternity, like Jesus, who knew that the cross was not the end of His story.

In the midst of all of this, in His moment of greatest need and loneliness, Jesus' friends left Him alone and fell asleep. It is easy to judge them, but don't. They are us. We are them. Has God ever caught you being lazy? Have you ever been caught sleeping on the job, spiritually speaking? Have you been guilty of fruitless faith? Who among us hasn't ever failed to be a faithful friend to Jesus? When we read the Bible, it can be tempting to put ourselves in the position of Jesus and see the failures of others toward us. But, before we use the Bible as binoculars to see their sin, we need to use it as a mirror to see our sin. Every one of us has had friends like Jesus' friends and been friends like Jesus' friends.

Humble prayer reminds us of this. We are weak, but God is strong, and His strength is perfected in our weakness. That's good news for those of us with bad resumes.

Jesus then arises to meet His pretend friend Judas, who betrays Him and has Him killed and buried. Three days later, Jesus roars back to life. For forty days, He appears to His followers and crowds of up to five hundred. Jesus was back in the pulpit! He began to give them final instructions before His ascension. What did He teach?

The Gethsemane Prayer.

We know this because nobody was there to hear Him pray this three-fold prayer. He was alone, and His disciples were asleep. So, He shared the details of those moments with them, teaching His prayer to them. It was so important that He wanted His followers to know what He prayed, how He felt, and what He said so we would learn from it and pray like it.

Reflection:

1. Can your friends count on you to persevere in prayer for them?
2. Describe any situation in your life where you struggle to pray, "Your will be done." Keep praying.

<u>NOTES</u>

PRAY LIKE JESUS

21-DAY DEVOTIONAL

DAY 12
GETHSEMANE PART 3: PRAY AGAINST TEMPTATION

Matthew 26:41 - "Watch and pray that you may not enter into temptation. The spirit indeed is willing, but the flesh is weak."

Jesus never had to pray for forgiveness since He didn't sin, but that doesn't mean He wasn't tempted. All of us are tempted, but like Jesus in the wilderness for 40 days being constantly tempted by Satan, we don't have to give in.

Too often we act out of our flesh or folly and then pray our apologies (which we should do!), but it is better to pray preemptively, guarding our hearts against temptation and asking God for wisdom.

In Matthew 26:41, Jesus says, "Watch and pray that you may not enter into temptation. The spirit indeed is willing, but the flesh is weak." We know that we have weak spots, places we drift away from God's will. We all have different appetites. Sex, food, alcohol, money, anger, work, etc. We should be praying that God would strengthen us in those areas, help us satisfy those appetites in godly ways, and steer us away from people and places and thoughts that tempt us to satisfy them in sinful ways.

Praying in advance guards us against our flesh and folly. This pattern of offensive prayer, before the battle is lost, is commonly found in the book of Psalms. On page after page, offensive prayers are recorded. They are written by people in the crucible of life, fearful for their well-being, exhausted, under assault, and weary.

In these prayers, the people of God remind themselves of the power and might of God, and ways in the past when He delivered His people. Frequent examples include the day in which God crushed the oppressors in Egypt and delivered his people from slavery into freedom by the might of his hand.

These kinds of offensive prayers are really what spiritual warfare is all about. In the middle of a battle for our life and soul, offensive prayer reminds us who our King is and invites Him to strengthen us and defend us. Even though little kids kneeling at their bedside praying with their grandmother may not look like soldiers, they are in fact at war in the spiritual realm.

This is the kind of prayer the Lord Jesus is asking you to pray – offensive prayers against the flesh and folly in advance before the battle is lost. Therefore, it is helpful to be honest about the ways and times you are most vulnerable to the flesh and folly. Then, you can pray offensively in advance and war against your flesh and folly by the power of God's Spirit like Jesus did.

Reflection:
1. What area(s) of your life are you weakest, most vulnerable, and easily tempted? Spend time today in prayer confessing those areas to God, asking forgiveness for ways in which you have fallen in these areas in the past.
2. Also, invite God the Spirit to help you practice self-control and self-discipline when these temptations arise.

21-DAY DEVOTIONAL

<u>NOTES</u>

PRAY LIKE JESUS

DAY 13
THE HIGH PRIESTLY PRAYER PART 1: PRAY FOR YOURSELF

John 17:1-5 - When Jesus had spoken these words, he lifted up his eyes to heaven, and said, "Father, the hour has come; glorify your Son that the Son may glorify you, since you have given him authority over all flesh, to give eternal life to all whom you have given him. And this is eternal life, that they know you, the only true God, and Jesus Christ whom you have sent. I glorified you on earth, having accomplished the work that you gave me to do. And now, Father, glorify me in your own presence with the glory that I had with you before the world existed.

Jesus' prayer in John 17 models life-changing, burden-lifting, hope-giving truth. This prayer is the longest recorded prayer we have from Jesus Christ. It is commonly referred to as Jesus' High Priestly Prayer because He takes the place of the High Priest entering the spiritual holy of holies through prayer, interceding for sinners before the Father.

This lengthy prayer does not appear in the synoptic Gospels (Matthew, Mark, and Luke) but is recorded in John's Gospel alone. Had John not included Jesus' prayer, we would be without any record of this great and vital moment in world history.

The first section of the prayer highlights Jesus praying for Himself.

21-DAY DEVOTIONAL

Some people struggle to pray for themselves for a variety of reasons. But if Jesus prayed for Himself and was perfect, it is perfectly good for you to do the same and pray for yourself. If you're struggling with how to do this, here are eight ways you can pray for yourself.

1. Pray to live "kingdom down": This world is not normal, home, or forever. We can look up to God or down on others. Truth, love, forgiveness, and servanthood are how we invite the Holy Spirit and heaven down into our lives. Lies, hatred, bitterness, and selfishness are how we pull unholy spirits and hell up into our lives.

2. Pray to deepen your relationship with God: Does God care about you? Yes: He's your Father! Does God listen to you? Yes: He's your Father! Does He want to help you? Yes: your Dad does!

3. Pray to prepare yourself for big changes: And as we learned in the Gethsemane Prayer, Jesus did not pray to get out of hardship; He prayed to get through it. For Christians, the way to keep going is to keep praying.

4. Pray to glorify God in all you do: We are God's mirror. When Genesis says we were made in God's "image," it means that when God looks at our lives, He should be able to see Himself reflected in our character and conduct.

5. Pray to exercise your authority: Positionally, we are in Christ. Practically, Christ is in us through the Holy Spirit. Being in Christ means that just as the Father has given authority to Christ, Christ has given authority to Christians. When we pray, we are inviting the unseen realm to flood our seen realm, bringing the

presence of God to empower our lives.

6. Pray to live in light of eternity: Some people are not interested in heaven because it sounds hellish to them. According to Jesus, eternal life is life with God. It is knowing God, being connected to God, enjoying a relationship with God. Sadly, when eternal life is seen only as a place, the focus on God is lost. The truth is that although heaven is a glorious place, it would be hell if God were not present there.

7. Pray to clarify God's will for you: God invites us to faithfulness, not busyness. Being like Christ does not mean keeping ourselves busy and asking God to bless our frantic lives. Instead, we need to start with prayer and discover what God's will is for us. Then we can say yes to what we should be doing by saying no to lots of other things we could be doing.

8. Pray to experience God's presence: Jesus tells us that in this life, we will suffer as He did. Therefore, our hope is not to escape suffering but to find God's will in the midst of it. If you cannot get out of tough circumstances, God's presence can get you through them, and that is exactly what Jesus asks the Father for.

Jesus models for us the truth that before we can live a life that glorifies God, we need to spend time in heartfelt prayer to know what will glorify God, and then receive the Spirit's power to press forward until God is glorified.

Reflection:

1. How about you? How should you be praying for yourself?
2. What opportunities has God given you to glorify Him, even by enduring hardship, pain, and injustice?
3. Do you know what God has called you to do? Are you doing it?

<u>NOTES</u>

PRAY LIKE JESUS

21-DAY DEVOTIONAL

DAY 14
THE HIGH PRIESTLY PRAYER PART 2: PRAY FOR CHRISTIANS

John 17:6-19 - "I have manifested your name to the people whom you gave me out of the world. Yours they were, and you gave them to me, and they have kept your word. Now they know that everything that you have given me is from you. For I have given them the words that you gave me, and they have received them and have come to know in truth that I came from you; and they have believed that you sent me. I am praying for them. I am not praying for the world but for those whom you have given me, for they are yours. All mine are yours, and yours are mine, and I am glorified in them. And I am no longer in the world, but they are in the world, and I am coming to you. Holy Father, keep them in your name, which you have given me, that they may be one, even as we are one. While I was with them, I kept them in your name, which you have given me. I have guarded them, and not one of them has been lost except the son of destruction, that the Scripture might be fulfilled. But now I am coming to you, and these things I speak in the world, that they may have my joy fulfilled in themselves. I have given them your word, and the world has hated them because they are not of the world, just as I am not of the world. I do not ask that you take them out of the world, but that you keep them from the evil one. They are not of the world, just as I am not of the world. Sanctify them in the truth; your word is truth. As you sent me into the world, so

PRAY LIKE JESUS

I have sent them into the world. And for their sake I consecrate myself, that they also may be sanctified in truth."

After praying for Himself, Jesus proceeds to pray for His followers who would come to believe in Him as God and would subsequently bring the good news of His person and work to the world.

Jesus prays for our keeping:

In our relationship with God, the wonderful news is that "if we are faithless, he remains faithful" (2 Timothy 2:13). Our God is rock steady in His love, devotion, and character. When we wander, He waits for us to return and never closes His heart toward us as Christians. Our Father loves us and is completely committed to "keeping" us. We maintain our relationship with God because God keeps us.

If you have a painful history with a ministry leader who completely abandoned the faith, the story of Judas is meant to provide clarity for you. If you have a loved one who has strayed from the Lord but you believe they are genuinely saved, the story of the prodigal son is meant to provide comfort for you.

Jesus prays for godly unity over demonic division:

God works through unity, and Satan works through division. There was no division until Satan chose to become independent, rebel, and cause division by recruiting angels to become demons in a coup attempt. On earth, Satan continues to recruit human beings to join the demons in their division against God.

However, unity does not mean uniformity. Like any family, God's family has a lot of diversity. Different Christians can have different

21-DAY DEVOTIONAL

methods for how they live their lives while maintaining unity on the principles behind them. In the church family, this unity is to be theological (what we believe), relational (how we love), missional (what we do), and organizational (how we coexist). The church is a big family, and like any big family, unity has to be the priority and comes at a cost.

Jesus prays for our joy:

Jesus' next words in this portion of the prayer are about joy. Simply put, the life of a Christian, like the life of Jesus, is not always marked by great comfort, wealth, health, ease, or simplicity. Nevertheless, it is filled with the presence of God and the purpose of God so that all we have, do, and endure can and will be used to glorify God and benefit others as it was with Jesus when He went to the cross.

Our joy is not found, then, by our current state in the world (that place of sin and rebellion against God), but rather by the presence and power of God in us even while we are in the world. For this, we rejoice because, for the Christian, this world is as close to hell as we will ever get, and we are almost home to heaven.

Jesus prays for our protection:

The world is marked with the life-damaging effects of sin and pain and death. One of the devil's most powerful lies is telling us joy is out there in the world. When you become a Christian, what was tempting in the world now strikes you as tragic. What you used to enjoy you are now ashamed of. What you used to brag about you now mourn. What you used to attend parades for, you now have funerals for. When God changed you, your relationship with the world changed, and He doesn't want it to change back.

PRAY LIKE JESUS

Jesus prays for our mission:

Jesus helps us figure out how to be good missionaries with His words on being in the world but not of it. Every area of the world needs missionaries, and all Christians need to be missionaries. Jesus loves the lost people who cross our paths, and He sent us to take His love to them.

For this reason, every Christian must love people, serve people, and engage people. Part of our mission in all corners of the world and its contexts means listening to people, empathizing, reading the literature, pounding the cultural pavement, even understanding the entertainment. We want to understand people because we are then best able to help them.

It is amazing to consider that on one of Jesus' darkest and most difficult days, He stopped to pray for you and the rest of us who are Christians. Even more amazing, Jesus continues to pray for us and is doing so right now. Jesus "is able to save to the uttermost those who draw near to God through him, since he always lives to make intercession for them," because, "Christ Jesus is the one who died—more than that, who was raised—who is at the right hand of God, who indeed is interceding for us" (Hebrews 7:25, Romans 8:34).

Right now, Jesus is aware of what you are going through, including the hopes you have, burdens you bear, and fears you face. Right now, Jesus is talking to the Father and Spirit along with angels and other divine beings about you as He intercedes for you. The High Priestly prayer continues every moment of every day and should be an incredible encouragement that you are loved, prayed for, and Someone is staying up all night concerned for you and interceding for you!

Reflection:
1. Do you currently pray for Christians? How can you improve in this practice?
2. Are you living in a way that is unified with fellow believers? How?
3. Are you a good missionary? What can you learn from Jesus about living on mission wherever God has put you?

NOTES

PRAY LIKE JESUS

21-DAY DEVOTIONAL

DAY 15
THE HIGH PRIESTLY PRAYER PART 3: PRAY FOR NON-CHRISTIANS

John 17:20-26 - "I do not ask for these only, but also for those who will believe in me through their word, that they may all be one, just as you, Father, are in me, and I in you, that they also may be in us, so that the world may believe that you have sent me. The glory that you have given me I have given to them, that they may be one even as we are one, I in them and you in me, that they may become perfectly one, so that the world may know that you sent me and loved them even as you loved me. Father, I desire that they also, whom you have given me, may be with me where I am, to see my glory that you have given me because you loved me before the foundation of the world. O righteous Father, even though the world does not know you, I know you, and these know that you have sent me. I made known to them your name, and I will continue to make it known, that the love with which you have loved me may be in them, and I in them."

Lastly, Jesus prays for those who didn't yet know Him. When Jesus prays, "I do not ask for these only, but also for those who will believe in me through their word..." He was praying for you. It is a bit staggering to consider that, with His own complex life to manage and death to endure that we were in His heart and on His mind.

Not only does Jesus model for us the importance of praying for lost people, He also prays for us to talk to lost people about Him as they come to "believe in me," Jesus says, "through their word." Jesus alone saves people, but you and I are sent to speak to people about Him.

God not only oversees the ends of things (who is saved) but also the means (how they are saved). Jesus prays for evangelism and unity because unity provides the power for mission. When a group of people unifies around a mission, willing to pay the price to complete it and stick together, big things can happen.

For this reason, not only does Jesus pray for people to become Christians, but He also prays for Christians to speak to non-Christians. Likewise, every Christian should, out of love, have a list of people they know and pray will become Christians. By praying for them, we are asking God the Holy Spirit to prepare them to hear about Jesus and prepare us to speak with them about Jesus.

One of the easiest ways to begin warming people up to Jesus is simply telling them you care and asking them whether there is anyone or anything you can be praying about for them. Most of the time, even a non-Christian appreciates someone regularly praying for their need, and this opens the door of an ongoing conversation about how they are doing and how you can lovingly support them. Eventually, these relationships that start with praying for someone will transition to conversations with them about Jesus.

Unlike the rest of us, Jesus Christ came down. For eternity, He sat on a throne, surrounded and served by divine beings including angels, had worship songs sung to Him, lacked nothing, needed nothing, had all power, all wealth, and all authority ruling over all Creation. Then, He gave it all up to come down to be with us, to be like us, and to serve us.

Jesus' riches-to-rags story seems a bit odd to those of us who are hoping that our lives will be a rags-to-riches story. Jesus' journey from glory to humility and back into glory sounds to us as foolishness, which the Bible says it is to some who hear it. While on the earth, theologians like to say that Jesus' glory was veiled so that we saw merely a humble, poor, powerless Galilean peasant.

Think of glory in terms of weightiness and majesty. Regarding weightiness, there are people and things in our life that matter most to us—meaning they outweigh other people and things. For the Christian, an example would be that the Bible outweighs all other books and that the relationship with your spouse outweighs all other human relationships.

Regarding majesty, something in us as created beings feels a sense of worshipful awe when we are in the presence of something far bigger and stronger than we are. For example, where we live in the desert of Arizona, when monsoon seasons arrive, massive clouds roll in, rain pours from the sky, and lightning lights up the night. The power and strength of a monsoon cause people to stop what they are doing and stand in awe at its power. Similarly, a few-hour drive north of us is the Grand Canyon. People from around the world travel to see what is basically a very large hole in the ground. Why? When you stand or sit on the edge, you feel incredibly small and insignificant—something surprisingly satisfying to the soul made for the glory of God's presence.

Jesus prayed that we would see Him in glory. When all is said and done and we are together forever, His prayer will be answered forever and ever. In the meantime, we live for God's glory until we see the God of glory. Jesus' prayer reminds us of four great truths about glory:

1. Our God is glorious. More powerful, wonderful, joyful, helpful, and incredible is our God than anyone or anything, or everyone and everything!

2. Our message is glorious. To have the great honor of telling people about the glorious love and grace of our great God and Savior, Jesus Christ, is an incredible honor. In a world filled with gory bad news, we get to tell people the good news of Jesus' glory!

3. Our mission is glorious. No matter where we go or what we do, the underlying mission is always the same for the Christian—to bring glory to God because God is glorious and alone worthy of glory. The Christian who eats their meal, washes their dishes, changes their baby, works their job, suffers their grief, forgives their enemy, and evangelizes their neighbor does it all to God's glory, which is the source of our joy!

4. Our future is glorious. One day there will be no more politicians or elections, tears or fears, or fights or funerals. One day, everyone and everything that belongs to Jesus will be together in glory, forever healed, unified, and glorified with Jesus forever.

Reflection:

1. Who prayed for you to become a believer? Write about your thankfulness for this person.
2. Which non-Christians can you start praying for?

21-DAY DEVOTIONAL

<u>NOTES</u>

PRAY LIKE JESUS

DAY 16
WHEN DID JESUS PRAY? PART 1

Deuteronomy 6:4 - "Hear, O Israel: The Lord our God, the Lord is one."

Mark 12:29-30 - Jesus answered, "The most important is, 'Hear, O Israel: The Lord our God, the Lord is one. And you shall love the Lord your God with all your heart and with all your soul and with all your mind and with all your strength.'"

Mark 1:35 - And rising very early in the morning, while it was still dark, he departed and went out to a desolate place, and there he prayed.

Now that we've dug into some examples of Jesus' prayer life, let's explore how to practically build a prayer life like His. Praying like Jesus means praying for just about everything: all needs, all situations, all people. If you want to pray like Jesus, it means you must also pray without ceasing. For disciples of Jesus, there is no acceptable prayerless time. Therefore, it's good to pray daily and pray early as Jesus did.

Jesus prayed daily

Jesus prayed every day. The Jews prayed the Shema daily–"Hear, O Israel: the LORD our God, the LORD is one" (Deuteronomy 6:4)–and as a devout Jew, Jesus would have done the same. This explains why He could quote it freely from memory in Mark 12:29-30.

As God incarnate, Jesus was a man who was perfectly integrated with the will of the Father, and maintaining conformity to the Father's will meant maintaining communication with the Father. Not a day went by that Jesus didn't pray, because every day He was faced with new temptations, trials, and tribulations that He needed to talk to the Father about.

Jesus prayed early

This is tough for the night owls to handle, but praying early in the morning is not only something Jesus did, it is something we should do too. Before the phone rings, before the inbox fills up, before the day gets hectic and busy, dedicate your day to the will of God before it starts running roughshod all over you.

Mark 1:35 tells us, "And rising very early in the morning, while it was still dark, he departed and went out to a desolate place, and there he prayed." While it was still dark. That's early.

Praying early, while your environment is still and quiet, gives you alone time with God without distractions. Such focus sets the tone for the rest of the day, preparing you for when your environment is frantic and loud.

Praying early calibrates us for all that lay ahead that day. And, it's a good way to spend the time devoted on our commute in preparation for the day ahead.

Reflection:

1. How often do you pray?
2. What is your most common time of the day to pray?
3. Are there any changes you need to make in these two areas?

PRAY LIKE JESUS

NOTES

21-DAY DEVOTIONAL

DAY 17
WHEN DID JESUS PRAY? PART 2

Matthew 14:19 - Then he ordered the crowds to sit down on the grass, and taking the five loaves and the two fish, he looked up to heaven and said a blessing. Then he broke the loaves and gave them to the disciples, and the disciples gave them to the crowds.

Mark 14:23 - And he took a cup, and when he had given thanks he gave it to them, and they all drank of it.

Luke 22:19 - And he took bread, and when he had given thanks, he broke it and gave it to them, saying, "This is my body, which is given for you. Do this in remembrance of me."

Just as food nourishes our body, so prayer nourishes our soul. And, praying over our meals combines the two so that our body and soul are nourished.

Jesus prayed at mealtime

Mealtime prayers seem to be going out of fashion, but even a quick survey of the Gospels will show Jesus continually praying over meals.

Jesus not only prayed that God would provide daily bread, He thanked God for the provision before He ate it. In Matthew 14:19 we read this:

PRAY LIKE JESUS

"Then he ordered the crowds to sit down on the grass, and taking the five loaves and the two fish, he looked up to heaven and said a blessing. Then he broke the loaves and gave them to the disciples, and the disciples gave them to the crowds."

Jesus understands that God is deserving of thanks for all provision, and he is intentional about thanking God for the provision of something you and I often take for granted – food. In some cultures, Christians pray at the end of the meal, thanking God especially for the parts they liked the best. That's fine too.

Most of you reading this live in a culture of abundance. Even if you do not have much money, chances are you don't go a day without food to eat and water to drink. When was the last time you thanked God for that "ordinary" provision? There are millions in the world who do not know if they will eat today. Perhaps thanking God at mealtime shouldn't be so perfunctory.

Jesus continually blesses "ordinary" meals, but he also blessed special meals. In Mark 14:23, we read, "And he took a cup, and when he had given thanks he gave it to them, and they all drank of it." And in Luke 22:19: "And he took bread, and when he had given thanks, he broke it and gave it to them, saying, 'This is my body, which is given for you. Do this in remembrance of me.'"

Don't pray the same thing every time! Don't be rote with your mealtime prayers. You may also want to be careful and thoughtful with what you pray. Often with good intentions, the prayer is uttered, "Lord bless this food to the nourishment of our bodies." But, that's exactly what He made it to do. It is a bit like praying, "Lord make this water wet."

Pray from your heart. Thank God for the particular food, thank God for the particular people who prepared it, and thank God for the particular people you're eating with.

Reflection:
1. Do you commonly pray over your meals in a meaningful way? If not, today is a good day to start.
2. Do you thank God for your daily provisions?

NOTES

PRAY LIKE JESUS

DAY 18
WHERE DID JESUS PRAY?

Luke 3:21 - Now when all the people were baptized, and when Jesus also had been baptized and was praying, the heavens were opened...

John 11:41-42 - So they took away the stone. And Jesus lifted up his eyes and said, "Father, I thank you that you have heard me. I knew that you always hear me, but I said this on account of the people standing around, that they may believe that you sent me."

Mark 11:7 - And they brought the colt to Jesus and threw their cloaks on it, and he sat on it.

Luke 9:28 - Now about eight days after these sayings he took with him Peter and John and James and went up on the mountain to pray.

Praying like Jesus means we should pray where Jesus prayed. And Jesus prayed anywhere and everywhere.

Jesus prayed publicly

Jesus prayed assertively in large groups on many different occasions. In fact, His public prayers nearly always were prayers for the public.

In Luke 3:21, He prays at a great special occasion: "Now when all the people were baptized, and when Jesus also had been baptized and was praying, the heavens were opened."

In John 11:41-42, Jesus raises Lazarus in front of a gawking crowd and then prays specifically about them: "So they took away the stone. And Jesus lifted up his eyes and said, 'Father, I thank you that you have heard me. I knew that you always hear me, but I said this on account of the people standing around, that they may believe that you sent me.'"

Jesus was not too shy to pray in public. He had a deep compassion people, so He prayed for them and in front of them as a witness to the mighty acts of God.

Jesus prayed corporately

As Jesus purified the temple, He offered the corrective found in Mark 11:17: "And he was teaching them and saying to them, 'Is it not written, "My house shall be called a house of prayer for all the nations?" But you have made it a den of robbers.'"

Jesus considered the place of corporate worship a place of prayer, and as He frequented the synagogues, He undoubtedly offered up prayers of petition and thanksgiving to the Father, whether He was teaching or not.

If the body of Christ prayed when He went to church, then the Body of Christ should pray when it goes to church. Prayer needs to be a part of the regular gathering of the local congregation. Prayer is integral to corporate worship.

Jesus prayed with others

Jesus not only prayed in large groups, He prayed in small groups, as in Luke 9:28: "Now about eight days after these sayings he took with him Peter and John and James and went up on the mountain to pray."

PRAY LIKE JESUS

There's Jesus' small group! Together, they went away to meet with each other and to meet with the Lord.

Small groups are vital to discipleship, because they teach you and train you for God-centered relationships with your brothers and sisters in Christ. As you pray with other believers, you learn how to pray and what to pray for. Sharing prayer requests, and praying for those requests together, helps create relationships of unity and empathy, which makes living life so much richer.

Reflection:
1. Find a person or group to pray with today, either in person or through technology (e.g. Skype or a phone call).

NOTES

21-DAY DEVOTIONAL

PRAY LIKE JESUS

DAY 19
HOW DID JESUS PRAY? PART 1

Mark 6:46 - And after he had taken leave of them, he went up on the mountain to pray.

Luke 5:15-16 - But now even more the report about him went abroad, and great crowds gathered to hear him and to be healed of their infirmities. But he would withdraw to desolate places and pray.

Mark 15:34 - And at the ninth hour Jesus cried with a loud voice, "Eloi, Eloi, lema sabachthani?" which means, "My God, my God, why have you forsaken me?"

Psalm 22:1 - My God, my God, why have you forsaken me? Why are you so far from saving me, from the words of my groaning?

Most of Jesus' prayer life is recorded to model for us methods of how to talk to the Father. Let's look at a few examples.

Jesus prayed alone

This is very, very important to the Christian life. Jesus prayed publicly in large and small groups, but He also prayed privately.

Mark 6:46 tells us, "And after he had taken leave of them, he went up on the mountain to pray." Luke 9:18 informs us that "...he was praying alone..."

21-DAY DEVOTIONAL

Sometimes being in the public for extended periods of time actually prompted Jesus to get away for a time, as in Luke 5:15-16: "But now even more the report about him went abroad, and great crowds gathered to hear him and to be healed of their infirmities. But he would withdraw to desolate places and pray."

Thousands are coming out to hear Jesus preach and teach, miracles are happening, healings are taking place. His ministry is powerful and therefore demanding. And He needed to get away for a bit to recharge and refresh.

He needed that. And you need that.

I think sometimes we forget what it's like to be alone with God because even when we are by ourselves, the noise of technology is drowning out our senses. The computer's on, the TV's on, the phone's on. We don't even know what silence sounds like anymore.

For me, I like to pray while I'm moving as I find my mind is clearer. So, I will go for a hike or take a drive in my Jeep with the top off and just talk to God aloud. Or, you can redeem your commute to or from work by turning off your technology and talking to God.

Most of us need to withdraw more frequently than we do to have a private meeting with God in prayer. I know that I have never taken this time and regretted it afterward.

Jesus prayed God's Word

Here is one stunning example from Mark 15:34: "And at the ninth hour Jesus cried with a loud voice, 'Eloi, Eloi, lema sabachthani?'" This lament is a direct quote from Psalm 22:1 and means, "My God, my God, why have you forsaken me?"

PRAY LIKE JESUS

Jesus, in this instance, is making the written revelation of God the verbal revelation of his prayer. This is a biblically shaped prayer life.

Bible study goes together like two oars in a boat. In prayer, we speak to God, and in Scripture God speaks to us.

Pray before you start reading. Pray as you're reading, thanking God for his Word and asking God to illuminate its meaning more brightly to you. Pray when you're done reading, and ask God to help you apply what you've read to your daily life.

Read and pray, read and pray, read and pray. Come in prayer to Scripture. When you read something convicting, stop and pray in repentance. When something impresses you, stop and praise God. When something reminds you of someone else, stop and pray for them.

The goal is not to just read through Scripture quickly to "get it over with," but to make reading Scripture an act of worship, an act of prayer. You may not get through passages quickly, but those passages will stick with you. And you'll enjoy your time in study more, because it will be shaping you in ways you can't imagine.

And if your prayer life is guided by Scripture, then you'll also know you will be praying in God's will.

Reflection:

1. Are you a regular Bible reader? If not, today is good day to find a Bible reading plan on the YouVersion app. As you read the Bible each day, stop to pray about what you read (e.g. for clear understanding, forgiveness, thanksgiving, other people, a practical need).

21-DAY DEVOTIONAL

NOTES

PRAY LIKE JESUS

DAY 20
HOW DID JESUS PRAY? PART 2

Luke 6:12 - In these days he went out to the mountain to pray, and all night he continued in prayer to God.

John 12:27 - "Now is my soul troubled. And what shall I say? 'Father, save me from this hour'? But for this purpose I have come to this hour."

Luke 23:46 - Then Jesus, calling out with a loud voice, said, "Father, into your hands I commit my spirit!" And having said this he breathed his last.

1 Thessalonians 5:18 - ...give thanks in all circumstances; for this is the will of God in Christ Jesus for you.

Matthew 11:25-26 - At that time Jesus declared, "I thank you, Father, Lord of heaven and earth, that you have hidden these things from the wise and understanding and revealed them to little children; yes, Father, for such was your gracious will."

Jesus' earthly life was perfect, which means he alone has the perfect prayer life. Therefore, there is no better way to learn about prayer than learning from the prayer life of Jesus.

21-DAY DEVOTIONAL

Jesus prayed long prayers

He didn't necessarily pray long prayers publicly, but Jesus spent lengthy amounts of time privately in prayer with the Father. Luke 6:12 gives us one example: "In these days he went out to the mountain to pray, and all night he continued in prayer to God."

In the heat of spiritual battle, Jesus went the distance. He prayed all night long. He was facing the decision over which men to pick as his disciples. That's serious business.

Many (perhaps most) times you should pray succinctly, but there are many times when the best thing you or I can do is get alone and go the distance in prayer. If you're facing a crisis or the imminence of a major life decision, I encourage you to get lots of time alone in prayer.

Before I married my wife Grace, I prayed long and hard. Before we have made major decisions about life and ministry, we have both prayed a ton both together and alone. In these times God helps us to process our thoughts, focus our desires, and come to clarity on his will for our lives so that we can move together confidently.

Jesus prayed thankful prayers

Perhaps the most common prayer Jesus prayed was a prayer of thanks. If you are interested in learning how to pray like Jesus, I can think of no better prayer habit for you to begin with than to, as Paul instructs in 1 Thessalonians 5:18, give thanks in all circumstances.

Here is one example from Jesus' prayer life, found in Matthew 11:25-26: "At that time Jesus declared, 'I thank you, Father, Lord of heaven and earth, that you have hidden these things from the wise and understanding and revealed them to little children; yes, Father, for such was your gracious will.'"

In this instance, Jesus is succinctly yet deeply thanking the Father for his gracious revelation of himself to us. It is a worshipful prayer, a theological prayer, and an insightful prayer, but it is first and foremost, a thankful prayer.

Do you want to begin building momentum in your prayer life? Perhaps you ought to begin by asking yourself, "What should I thank God for?" The answers to that question are endless, so get started and don't stop.

When you do that – as you do that – it builds inside of you hope and anticipation and expectation. It will make you a God-seeker and a grace-giver. It will open your heart to be searching for reasons to thank God and open your heart with joy for His many provisions. Thankful people are prayerful people.

Jesus prayed with his dying breath

In Luke 23:46, we read, "Then Jesus, calling out with a loud voice, said, 'Father, into your hands I commit my spirit!' And having said this he breathed his last." Jesus' final prayer at the moment of death was an incredible declaration of submission to the Father. In this moment, Jesus devotes his dying breath to the glory of God.

My prayer for you and for myself is that, as the culmination of a life lived in honor of God, we will honor God with our last breaths. May the name of the Lord be on our lips in the last words we speak. Not in cursing and not in bargaining, but in submission to the Father's will and in praise of His glorious grace. To prepare for that day, we need to be in prayer every day since we truly do not know when our last day will be.

21-DAY DEVOTIONAL

Reflection:

1. Make it a point to pray a short prayer every time something happens today for which you are thankful. See if this does not improve your attitude and also build momentum in your prayer life as you continue this habit in the days and months ahead.
2. Is there anything painful or fearful in your life right now that you need to spend extended time with God in prayer for, to work through with deep emotional processing? If so, when and how will you carve out this important time to meet with God?

<u>NOTES</u>

21-DAY DEVOTIONAL

DAY 21
CONCLUSION

Matthew 18:3 - ...and said, "Truly, I say to you, unless you turn and become like children, you will never enter the kingdom of heaven."

Our prayer for you is that this plan has helped you get a better grasp on why prayer is important and how Jesus modeled it for us through both His own prayers and teachings on prayers. Prayer is something we all grow in through the course of our walks with Jesus, so no matter where you're starting, He wants to help you keep going.

As you finish this plan, reflect on what you've learned and what next steps God is calling you to take to grow closer to Him through prayer.

God is a Father who wants to talk to, hear from, and help His kids. If you've enjoyed this plan and would like more resources about prayer, please visit **realfaith.com**. There you will find the full-length book from which this plan was derived, daily devotionals about prayer, sermons, and more.

Reflection:
1. What aspects of prayer has God highlighted for you to grow in after reading this plan?
2. How can you practically make plans to build good prayer habits (i.e. buy a prayer journal, find someone to practice praying with, block out

time in your schedule)?

3. How has your view of God the Father and prayer changed after reading this plan?

<u>NOTES</u>

21-DAY DEVOTIONAL

ABOUT PASTOR MARK DRISCOLL, ASHLEY CHASE & REAL FAITH

With Pastor Mark, it's all about Jesus! Mark and his wife Grace have been married and doing vocational ministry together since 1993. They also planted The Trinity Church with their five kids in Scottsdale, Arizona as a family ministry (thetrinitychurch.com) and started Real Faith, a ministry alongside their daughter Ashley that contains a mountain of Bible teaching from Pastor Mark as well as content for women, men, parents, pastors, leaders, Spanish-speakers and more.

Pastor Mark has been named by *Preaching Magazine* one of the 25 most influential pastors of the past 25 years. He has a bachelor's degree in speech communication from the Edward R. Murrow College of Communication at Washington State University as well as a master's degree in exegetical theology from Western Seminary in Portland, Oregon. For free sermons, answers to questions, Bible teaching, and more, visit **RealFaith.com** or download the **Real Faith app**.

As the oldest of the Driscoll kids, Ashley was born into ministry with her parents and has loved serving alongside them ever since. This is her first publication with her dad, and prayer is a topic especially close to her heart. She has studied theology at Capernwray Bible School in Costa Rica and attended Arizona State University, where she was involved with a 24/7 prayer tent that opened her eyes to prayer in relationship with the Father.

If you have any prayer requests for us, questions for future Ask Pastor Mark or Dear Grace videos, or a testimony regarding how God has used this and other resources to help you learn God's Word, we would love to hear from you at **hello@realfaith.com**.

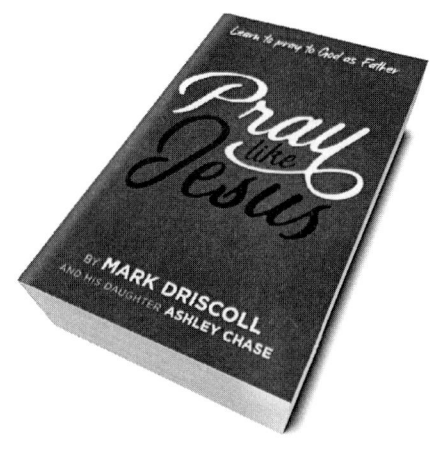

GET YOUR COPY OF "PRAY LIKE JESUS", THE FULL-LENGTH TITLE FROM WHICH THIS DEVOTIONAL IS ADAPTED FROM AT **REALFAITH.COM/STORE**

WANT MORE DEVOTIONAL PLANS FROM PASTOR MARK ON YOUVERSION?

DOWNLOAD THE YOUVERSION BIBLE APP ON IOS AND ANDROID.